Pebble® Plus

Let's Celebrate

Martin Luther King Jr. Day

JANUARY

by Clara Cella

Consulting Editor: Gail Saunders-Smith, PhD

CAPSTONE PRESS
a capstone imprint

Pebble Plus is published by Capstone Press,
1710 Roe Crest Drive, North Mankato, Minnesota 56003.
www.capstonepub.com

Library of Congress Cataloging-in-Publication Data
Cella, Clara.
Martin Luther King Jr. Day / by Clara Cella.
p. cm. — (Pebble plus. Let's celebrate)
Includes index.
Summary: "Full-color photographs and simple text provide a brief introduction to Martin Luther King Jr. Day"—
Provided by publisher.
ISBN 978-1-4296-8733-1 (library binding)
ISBN 978-1-4296-9388-2 (paperback)
ISBN 978-1-62065-307-4 (ebook PDF)
1. King, Martin Luther Jr., 1929–1968—Juvenile literature. I. Title.

E185.97.K5C44 2013
394.261—dc23   2012003826

Editorial Credits
Jill Kalz, editor; Kyle Grenz, designer; Marcie Spence, media researcher; Kathy McColley, production specialist

Photo Credits
Alamy: Picture Contact BV, 11; BigStockPhoto.com: adelaidecrow, 13; Capstone Studio: Karon Dubke, 7, 17, 19, 22;
   Corbis: Bettmann, cover, 5, Flip Schulke, 9, Nelvin C. Cepeda/ZUMA Press, 1, Susan Stocker/ZUMA Press, 15;
   Shutterstock: Losevsky Pavel, 21

Note to Parents and Teachers

The Let's Celebrate series supports curriculum standards for social studies related to culture.
This book describes and illustrates the Martin Luther King Jr. Day holiday. The images support
early readers in understanding the text. The repetition of words and phrases helps early readers
learn new words. This book also introduces early readers to subject-specific vocabulary words,
which are defined in the Glossary section. Early readers may need assistance to read some
words and to use the Table of Contents, Glossary, Read More, Internet Sites, and Index sections
of the book.

Printed in the United States   4512

Table of Contents

Hello, MLK Jr. Day!. 4

How It Began. 10

Let's Celebrate! 16

Activity: The Gift of Food 22

Read More 23

Internet Sites. 23

Glossary 24

Index 24

Hello, MLK Jr. Day!

Dr. Martin Luther King Jr. was a brave leader. He helped lead the civil rights movement. Americans honor him on Martin Luther King Jr. Day.

Martin Luther King Jr. Day
is a national holiday.
It is on the third Monday
of January. Government offices
and schools are closed that day.

Dr. King dreamed of a world without racism. People still celebrate that dream today by helping others and working for peace.

How It Began

Martin Luther King Jr.

grew up in a time of segregation.

Black people had fewer rights

than white people.

PUBLIC SWIMMING POOL

PUBLIC SWIMMING POOL
WHITE ONLY

SELMA, ALA

14 JULY 31

DRINKING FOUNTAIN

WHITE   COLORED

TGOMERY, ALA

14 JULY 31

REST ROOMS

Aug. 2, 1926   WHITE ONLY

COLORED
SEATED IN REAR

CO.

AUGUST 1, 1929

SHOWERS

White EM   Colored EM

DEPT. OF THE ARMY

FORM # 11734

Dr. King worked to change
unfair laws through peaceful ways.
Some people disagreed with him.
In 1968 he was shot and killed.

Martin Luther King Jr. Day was first celebrated in 1986. Across the country people walked in peace marches and listened to speeches.

15

Let's Celebrate!

It's Martin Luther King Jr. Day!

How will you celebrate?

Get to know your neighbors.

Have a block party

or a neighborhood walk.

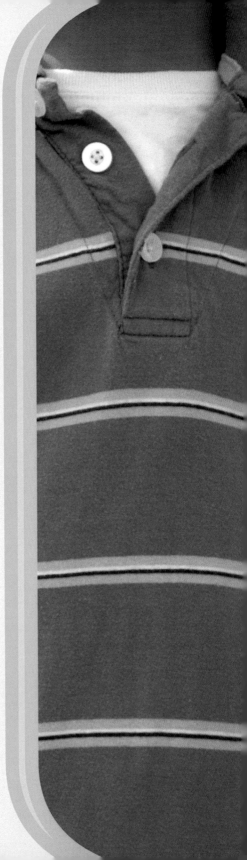

Help others. Volunteer to walk a neighbor's dog. Offer to rake leaves or shovel the sidewalk. Collect supplies for your school.

Make the world a better place for the future. Plant trees. Pick up litter. Follow Dr. King's example and treat others kindly and fairly.

Activity: The Gift of Food

Martin Luther King Jr. Day is a time to help others. Make sure people have enough to eat. Collect food for your local food bank.

What You Need:

an adult   a few friends   paper   markers

What You Do:

1. Have an adult take you and your friends to the local food bank. Ask workers there what kinds of food are needed.

2. Make flyers. Include who you are and why you are collecting food. Include a list of needed items. Also include when you'll be collecting.

3. With an adult, hand out the flyers to your neighbors.

4. On collection day pick up the food, and take it to the food bank. Don't forget to thank people who give!

Food Collection

Food Collection will benefit Parkstone Foodshelf.

Collection Date: March 19

Collection Time: 5:00 PM

Leave donated items by door

Items needed:
Juice Boxes
Canned Meals
Pasta
Rice
Canned Fruit
Canned Beans
Baby Food
Peanut Butter
Cereal
Soups

Thank you in advance!

Read More

Dayton, Connor. *Martin Luther King Jr. Day.* American Holidays. New York: PowerKids Press, 2012.

Miller, Reagan. *Martin Luther King, Jr. Day.* Celebrations in My World. New York: Crabtree Pub. Co., 2009.

Rissman, Rebecca. *Martin Luther King, Jr. Day.* Holidays and Festivals. Chicago: Heinemann Library, 2011.

Internet Sites

FactHound offers a safe, fun way to find Internet sites related to this book. All of the sites on FactHound have been researched by our staff.

Here's all you do:

Visit *www.facthound.com*

Type in this code: 9781429687331

 **Super-cool stuff!** Check out projects, games and lots more at **www.capstonekids.com**

Glossary

celebrate—to honor someone or something on a special day

civil rights movement—an effort in the 1950s and 1960s to get equal rights for all people

peace—a time without war or fighting

racism—the act of judging people unfairly based on their skin color

segregation—separating people because of their skin color

volunteer—to offer to do something without pay

Index

activities, 8, 14, 16, 18
closings, 6
dates, 6

Dr. King's
death, 12
dreams, 8
life, 4, 10, 12
history of holiday, 14

Word Count: 202
Grade: 1

Early-Intervention Level: 21